HEALING RITUAL MAGIC

Published by Ra Sekhi Arts Temple

By Kajara Nia Yaa Nebthet

First Edition Sept 2020

Cover Design by Jahaan London

ISBN 9798670945349

Copyright 2020

All rights reserved. This book, or parts thereof, may not be used or reproduced in any form without permission.

I dedicate this book to the sick,
depressed and oppressed people
of the world. Now is our time to
heal our minds, bodies and hearts.

Table of Contents

Foreword	4
Healing Magic	7
Rituals & Spiritual Power	9
Tools for Rituals	11
Times for Doing Rituals	16
Moon Phases & Seasons	18
Release Ritual	22
Heart Healing Ritual	30
Healing From Sexual Trauma Ritual	39
Womb Healing Ritual	48
Men's Healing Ritual	56
Relationship Elevation Ritual	67
Family Elevation Ritual	74
Ancestral Elevation Ritual	80
Prosperity Ritual	85
Manifestation Ritual	91
Hex/Spell Breaker Ritual	97
Freedom Ritual	102
Final Thoughts	108

Forward

A ritual is an action that is done in a certain order to produce specific results. Rituals are done to bring a change or shift in energy or to maintain balance. Rituals usually include certain physical movements, words, and other elements.

Rituals, when done correctly, can create more harmony and positive energy in our lives. We can use rituals to make our everyday activities more spiritual. For example, we can add prayers, songs, or affirmations when we shower, cook, or get dressed to go out to make the normally-mundane activity more spiritual.

Our thoughts, words and intentions add energy to everything that we do so adding the right elements directs the process in a particular way. Because energy is based on your feelings and intentions, rituals can be positive or negative. Be mindful of your energy before performing any ritual because your energy will influence the outcome. Making our lives more spiritual and ritualistic brings power and purpose to every aspect of our lives, from the mundane tasks to other more important experiences. For example if you are dealing with a physical sickness or disease you can perform a healing ritual to assist in your healing process. This will bring the spiritual realm into the physical healing process which we call wholistic healing.
The rituals included in this book are meant to help you learn how

to use natural and affordable supplies to bring balance and spiritual power to your life. I suggest using spiritual baths and altars to assist with your rituals. Each altar should be created for each particular ritual and should be taken down three months to a year after performing the ritual. You can pay attention to your feelings and look for results of your ritual work to know when to release the altar.

Working with Spirit and doing rituals requires that you learn to pay attention to your feelings and intuition so that you do what is best for you. You may get strong feelings or thoughts to do things a certain way. You may follow and do what feels right for you. Learn to pay attention and to be confident in your feelings. You have them for a reason.

Remember that spiritual work moves on a subtle energy field so you may not see the results of your work right away. It may take a few weeks or months to see the results of the ritual. Just know that after you do your part it is done and you just have to be patient at that point. Make sure to be thankful for the work happening the way you want it too, Doubt, worry and other negative emotions can effect your results. Be confident that the Universe will do it's part and that all is working in divine order.

These rituals were created to assist in your healing process. You will use sound, candles, incense, song, dance, prayers, symbols, focus, affirmations, and more in these rituals. They will help to shift the energy to create a proper frequency for the desired outcome.

Rituals can be done alone or in groups. Ritualistic meditations work best when you have someone to read them to you, or you can get our recordings of the meditations and listen to them when you are ready to perform the ritual.

Throughout this book, we will provide you with rituals you can conduct in your own home to enhance various parts of your life. Though each ritual comes with specific meditations, feel free to change the language as needed. They are written for your convenience so that you may perform them alone or with others. The user should feel open to modify them as needed to make them more useful to you.

You can safely do ritual work on behalf of those you are connected to through blood (mother, father, sister, brother, children, etc.), however you must get permission before doing rituals for those outside of your direct family lineage. You can always send love and positive energy to others, but to do a full ritual, reading, or healing session on someone without their permission is a misuse of energy and could come back to the doer in a number of negative ways. There is always reciprocity and an exchange of energy for everything that is put out into the universe. Keep this in mind before you do any spiritual ritual work.

HEALING MAGIC

We are living in a time where there is much healing needed. Many of us have experienced trauma or sickness in our lives or we are hurting or angry about experiences from our past. We may suffer from this hurt with pain in our bodies or hearts. Yet we do not often realize the connection between our thoughts and our pain. We may take our problems to others for them to fix us or help us. When we do this, we take the power away from ourselves. We may know how to do some limited things to heal our physical body, however wholistic healing requires us to heal each aspect of ourselves which includes healing our minds (mental), bodies (physical), hearts (emotional) and our souls (spiritual).

When we experience trauma, we must go through a healing process in order to become whole and balanced once again. The process is very similar to the process that our bodies go through when healing from a wound. There is a time when the wound is open: this is equivalent to when we are very emotional about the hurtful situation. As wound closes the skin becomes tough to protect the sore spot. It forms a scar, a mark to remind you of the pain. In the same way we become numb to the process as we allow our minds and hearts to resolve the issues in some way. The most common reaction is to try to forget about our pain or emotions so that we can continue to work or function without breaking down. We become hard like the scar formed over the sore that is healing underneath. Eventually the scar tissue begins to heal and the pain goes away physically, however when it comes to emotional healing it usually takes more than time to heal our wounds. Words may be forgotten but the feelings could linger and should be resolved for true healing to occur.

Sometimes we may numb our hearts so we don't feel the emotions, or the pain of the wound. These are defense mechanisms that we use in order to continue to work and take care of our families or responsibilities. However, these habits do not allow us to learn lessons nor change the emotions that we may have within.

In order to truly heal we have to do intentional work to release the emotions, to find a solution, or forgive ourselves and others. We have to express our emotions and shift our perspectives in for true healing to occur. We have to face our problems and learn lessons from hurtful experiences to heal, grow and change.

Traditionally, our ancestors used ritual magic to assist in the physical and emotional healing process. They understood that healing should be wholistic and should include all aspects of the self, otherwise it would not be complete. They understood that our power is in using natural things, rituals and spiritual power to encourage healing within families and individuals.

Our magic is in using our traditional ways of healing to promote wholistic healing of our minds, bodies, and spirits. We can accomplish this just as our ancestors did so many years ago. True healing requires the agreement of the mind and heart to go from a lesser state to a higher state of being. As we heal ourselves, we are also healing our families, children, ancestors, and those around us.

We can create a chain-reaction of healing by starting the process as an individual. That is the magic and power that we possess in this process; when we make up our minds to heal internally, the universe will align with us to assist with our journey. Healing magic can occur suddenly or gradually over time. Just remember to do your part to heal yourself, do the best that you can with what you know, where you are and what you have and then trust that the process is in motion. Now you just have to trust and allow the process to work for you. Stay in tune with yourself, be true to yourself and be gentle with yourself as the healing occurs.

RITUALS & SPIRITUAL POWER

Rituals bring spiritual power to the physical realm. Everything in the physical realm is created with thoughts, words, feelings and energy. When we combine certain elements like air, fire, water and earth we can create a spiritual ritual that will bring the energy needed to make miracles, changes and healing happen.

you in creating healing in your family or household. The rituals are made stronger by having the elements and energy needed. Lastly, the last thing required for them to work properly is spiritual power.

Spiritual power, sometimes referred to as Ase (Ashe) or Sekhem, is power that is gained from one's personal spiritual connection and practice. You could be born with spiritual power if your parents cultivated their spiritual power when you were conceived or during your childhood. Everyone is born with life force energy, but spiritual power is either inherited from your bloodline or cultivated through years of spiritual development and practice.

Those with spiritual power are better equipped to facilitate rituals in the correct way because they have developed a relationship with spirit and have usually been trained to work with spiritual forces correctly.

For this reason, we encourage you to cultivate your own spiritual power or consult with a Priest or Priestess for some of the more challenging rituals in this book. It is good to have someone who knows how to work with higher forces to assist you when doing spiritual work so that you can avoid mistakes and accidents.

Tools for Rituals

We use many tools in our rituals to bring the elements and energy needed to create the energy we want. Here are some items we use and why we use them in our rituals.

Candles

Energy: Fire, known for transformation, healing, purification, and change

Type: Using colored candles adds the energy of that particular color to the ritual

Type to Use: Tea lights, 7-day (in glass), pillar, or small pillar

Additional: Use natural unscented candles for rituals (scented candles made be made with unnatural ingredients)

CRYSTALS - Crystals are created with years of shifts and changes in the earth; therefore, they carry earth energy. They are helpful because they have certain minerals and they radiate energy based on the mineral content and the color of the crystal. Some crystals you may choose to work with are:

Amethyst for healing mind, body and spirit

Clear quartz to raise the frequency

Rose quartz for love and heart healing

Black tourmaline to absorb negative energy

Shungite to purify the environment

Jade for love and heart healing

Aventurine for healing relationships, heart and physical healing.

Malachite for attracting love and money,

Emerald to attract love, money and power.

Bloodstone for physical healing and motivation.

Turquoise for intuition and protection.

Citrine for clearing, purification and power.

WATER— water is known as a powerful element for healing, cleansing, clearing, purification and connecting to the ancestral and spiritual realms. Use pure,

Filtered water can be used in all rituals.

Tap water can be boiled first to purify it.

Spring water to make things come quickly.

Rain water for cleansing and spiritual power.

River water for things to flow constantly and consistently.

Sea water to add spiritual power and powerful healing.

INCENSE - Incense is used as aromatherapy. Some incense such as sage and frankincense are good to clear the air of toxins and as well as to clear the spiritual energy in a room or from a person. Some fragrances dissipate negative energy and some invoke or attract higher light energy. Some incense you may choose to use are Use resins or herbs with charcoal for best results. Wood incense may contain harsh chemicals.

Frankincense is known to call the higher forces.

Lavender for peace and calm energy.

Myrrh is known to call the ancestors.

Dragons blood for purification of negative energy.

Rose for love, peace and money.

Sandalwood for peace, meditation and healing.

Cedar for prosperity and strength.

Cinnamon for joy, harmony and prosperity.

ALTARS - Altars create a focal point for the energy that you are working with. They should be kept clean and sacred.

Those who did not create the altar should not touch the items on your altar unless directed by the creator of the altar.

When you create an altar, you should sprinkle a little water on it to activate it. Keep the altar clean and clear of dust and clutter. The more you use it, the more active it becomes.

An altar should become a portal to the spiritual realm for you and your household, so be mindful of the energy and words you speak around your altar.

Use a small table for your altar and make sure to keep it clean.

WORDS OF POWER - In spiritual work, your words help to activate the energy that you intend to balance or change.

Prayers and chants are examples of words of power. When you speak words into the universe, it directs the energy towards the energy you speak of

Spells are words that are brought together to encourage a certain frequency or vibration.

Affirmations are words used to reprogram or create a certain energy within and outside of you. . They become words of power. You can create your own words of power or use the ones we have shared with you.

COLORS - Colors are helpful in healing rituals because they vibrate at a certain frequency, and each color has specific properties. Use this information to help you choose the right colors to use for your healing work. Use the colors prescribed for each ritual or choose a different one that feels right for the purposes of your ritual. Read the properties of each color below:

Black: absorbs and removes negative energy. Good for breaking blockages and stagnant energy.

Blue: for healing, peace, harmony and spiritual inspiration.

Yellow: for joy, wisdom, luck, good fortune and mental power.

Green: for balance, healing, good fortune and success.

Orange: for movement, change, happiness, energy and stimulation.

Purple: for psychic power, spiritual wisdom and power, high vibrations.

Pink: for healing, to banish negativity and depression.

Red: for strength, heat, energy, courage, good health, will power.

White: for balance, spiritual power, healing, purification.

SOUND THERAPY - We can use meditative music, or binary tones to enhance our rituals. Both can be found online. You can also use drums, singing bowls or other instruments as well.

INTENTIONS- Your thoughts and intentions are most important for these or any other rituals to work. You must focus on the work you are doing and not allow others' thoughts to consume your energy while performing the rituals. Stay focused and keep your intentions pure and sincere for the best results. Remember: every thought and word that you put out into the universe will come back to you, positively or negatively. It is good to write down your intentions before you do the rituals to help you direct and focus you energy and thoughts.

INTEGRITY - Do each ritual with the most integrity. Do not harbor ill feelings or harmful intentions when doing healing work.

Spirit Guides - You have Spirit Guides that can assist you in your healing process. You can call on THE MOST HIGH, your Ancestors, your Spirit Guides, Deities, Angels or other forces to assist with your rituals.

CLEANLINESS - Make sure to clean your environment physically and smudge (burn incense) your space with sage or frankincense before doing any spiritual or healing work. Cleanliness is next to Godliness!

Best Times for Doing Rituals

Choose a specific day and time to do your rituals to add the power of the universe or more spiritual power to your work. Each day has a certain energy and the time of day for doing ritual work is just as important to the ritual working the way that it is meant to. Make sure to also tune in to the moon cycles when you plan your rituals. For example, you do not want to perform a prosperity ritual during a time when the moon is waning because that is the time when the moon is getting dark or smaller to the eye to see so the energy of the moon will work with you to take things away. Do a ritual to gain something when the energy of the moon is increasing. Understand that doing rituals on the proper day and time will add power to your ritual.

Days of the Week

Mondays are good for rituals concerning women, fertility, growth, abundance, healing, relationships, family.

Tuesdays are good for doing rituals for men, for banishing, releasing, fighting enemies, protection, growth, expansion.

Wednesdays are good for things dealing with communication, intelligence, opening the way, mental activities, movement, meetings, messages.

Thursdays are good for rituals concerning relationships, career, money, luck, prosperity, wealth, health, expansion, growth.

Fridays are good for rituals concerning relationships, beauty, wealth, love, joy, success, abundance.

Saturday is a good day for doing rituals to releasing, mysteries, growth, change, transformation.

Sundays are good for doing rituals for spiritual growth, elevation, spiritual power, change, transformation, healing.

TIMES OF THE DAY

Choose the time of day for your ritual based on the what your are working to achieve and the energy required to make it work.

Mornings

Mornings are good to do rituals that are adding to something or to increase the energy. as the sun rises, so does the energy of the day. For example if you want to attract money do the ritual early.

Afternoon

Noon is the sun is at the highest point in the sky and the energy is strong and vibrating at a high frequency. This is a powerful time for most rituals. When the sun begins to set the energy shifts to that of decreasing or taking away.

Evening/ Night

As the day moves into night and darkness sets in the time for doing rituals concerning shadow work or to break negative energy patterns is powerful. After 10 pm the energy is said to be ruled by the underworld or more malevolent forces until around two or three in the morning so be careful to not perform certain rituals during this time.

MOON PHASES AND SEASONS

You may want to also consider the moon when doing rituals as well. The moon has a feminine energy and effects our personal feminine energy in different ways. You may notice, that you become more emotional during or around the full moon times. This is a time when people tend to argue and have accidents more because of the influence of the moon. If you are unbalanced spiritually, mentally or emotionally it can affect you even more. When you are aware of the influence and the phases of the moon you can prepare and behave accordingly.

New Moon

The new moon is a time when the energy of our planet is being renewed. Ones would say cut your hair on the new moon to ensure it will grow again, back in the day. So it is a time for doing things that you want to increase or add to. Setting intentions for new beginning and new projects is good during this time.

Waxing Moon

As the moon is waxing or growing this is a good time to do rituals for growth, regeneration, healing, prosperity, attraction and relationships.

Full Moon

Full moon time is a powerful time for doing most rituals. The energy of the moon is fully charged and can be used for prosperity, releasing, healing, family, relationships, and more.
We recommend doing full moon rituals outside under the moon for best results. During rituals at night during a full moon is powerful.

Waning Moon

As the moon begins to shed until it becomes dark the time for doing shadow work, releasing, breaking spells and hexes and that type work.

We do not encourage anyone to do dark work against others. Remember that it is spiritually immoral to do work against the will of others. Doing such dark work will come with a price, karma and reciprocity will come into action with all rituals.

Seasons

You may also want to consider the seasons when doing long term rituals such as family healing. Each season has a particular energy and element that it is associated with.

Winter is associated with Earth and earth rituals. It is a good time for silence, healing, regeneration, planning, and building.
Spring is a time of renewal and regeneration. It is associated with water, therefore water rituals are powerful to do during the spring. Growth, regeneration and fertility rituals are

powerful to do during the spring.

Summer is an active, high energy time as the days are longer and the sun is hotter. This is a fire element time and fire rituals are very powerful during the summer. This is also a good time for growth, prosperity, cleansing and abundance rituals.

Fall is associated with the air element and is a good time for releasing rituals, as the trees begin to release the leaves from the trees. This is a good time for healing, purification, releasing and manifestation rituals.

The rituals in this book bring those elements together to assist with your overall healing.

THE RITUALS

The Release Ritual

Living on planet Earth at this time is full of challenging experiences and tests. We all suffer from some loss, illness or other experience that can make us heavy and bitter. We have been through experiences that cause us to build up emotions like fear, anger, worry and doubt.

When we don't know how to process our emotions they can become overwhelming and create havoc in our current situations. this ritual is perfect for those who have experienced trauma, drama and heartbreak. It can be helpful for those who are holding emotions (fear, anger, sadness, etc....) or have suffered abuse and/or loss.

Negative emotions can get stuck in our minds and bodies when we don't find a way to release them. We can talk it out, dance it out, shake, sing, cry, shout, paint, draw, make music or do something creative to express those feelings. Many people use drugs, alcohol, food, sex, TV, people and other things to keep them from dealing with or feeling their pain. These are unhealthy ways of dealing with our feelings. Doing spiritual rituals are healthy ways of dealing with our emotions.

This ritual can was created to help ones in releasing negative energy from the mind, body and spirit. It uses a combination of sound therapy, discussion, meditation and aura clearing to help one release and find peace within. It will create a shift to allow ones to bring things to the surface so they can be resolved and released completely.

This ritual can be done alone or within a group. Wear white for best results.

It can be performed on Monday, Tuesday, Thursday, Friday or Sunday.

ITEMS NEEDED:

- Singing bowl
- Drum or rattle
- Clearing incense (benzoin, sage, dragon's blood, frankincense)
- White or purple candle
- Binary tones 432 mgh and up
- Paper
- Pen
- Yoga Mat
  Container for burning
- Charcoal
- White cloth for the altar
-

The Ritual:

Always make sure to physically clean your space before doing any ritual or spiritual work.

1. Start with smudging the space and aura of each participant. Take your incense resins or sage and walk around the house in a counterclockwise direction to release negative energy from the space. Take the incense around the participants in a counterclockwise direction to help clear energy from their auric field.

2. Light your candle. state your intentions out loud for the ritual while lighting the candle.

3, Pour libation and call on your righteous ancestors and Spirit Guides for protection. Say the names of your ancestors while you pour water on the floor or on the ground for each name. You can call on Angels or other Forces to help you as well.

4. Take a moment to think and speak about the importance of releasing negative emotions. We are meant to feel, but we are not meant to walk around holding negative emotions for long periods of time.

5. Next we will do some tapping of the minor and major aritu (chakras) to allow the body to be open to release. Tap using the first two fingers on each hand. Lightly touch each point mentioned four or five times to activate the energy. Start with the top of your head. Then move down to your first eye, temples, throat, heart, shoulders, elbows, solar plexus (under rib cage), under the navel and lower back. You can tap the hips, knees and feet as well to release stagnant energy you may be holding in those areas.

6. After the tapping process, stand up and shake the body to shake and clear away negative energy. Shake your head, arms, legs, hips, and release any stagnant energy that you are holding.

7. Sweep your aura using your hands by moving down the front of your body, then your back and under your arms and feet. Shake

the energy from your body out of a window or door. Imagine that it will be turned into something beautiful.

8. Turn on your binary tones and sit down to write about the things, people, feelings and everything that you want to release.

9. Use the following starting with your name:

I (your name) ask the universe (or Creator) to help me release

(write your list of the things, people, or feelings you want to release)

So be it and so it is from this day forward.

It is done.

Thank you Great Spirit, Universe, Ancestors and Spirit Guides

10. When you are finished with your list, Fold the paper away from you (to take the energy in the opposite direction) and keep folding it until you have a small little square.

11. Put the paper in the burning pot with the sage and light it. Let it burn until the paper burns all the way out. As you light and burn the paper, say: "Thank you for the release and healing that is taking place". Know that your words, emotions and energy are being transformed by the fire and carried into the ethers.

12. When you feel ready after the ritual, recite these affirmations aloud. You should say them at least three times each. Say them with meaning and add your own if needed.

RELEASE AFFIRMATIONS

I release the negative energy from past lifetimes.
I release the blocks from past lifetimes.
I release the karma from past life times.
I release all negative energy from my ancestors.
I release the blocks from my ancestors.
I release all karma from my ancestors.
I release the negative energy from my childhood.
I release the negative experiences from my childhood.
I release the abuse, neglect and negative energy from my parents.
I release the negative words and energy from my family.
I release the karma from my parents and family.
I release all negative emotions and energy from past relationships.
I release all negative ties, oaths, commitments and bonds that do not serve me.
I release all fear, doubt, worry, guilt, shame, regret, jealousy, sadness and anger.
I release bitterness and frustration, disappointments, disagreements or other negative energy that has been holding me down.
I release stress and sickness from my mind, heart and body.
From this day forward.
So be it and so it is. I give thanks
Ase Amen RA Maat

13. Sweep your aura again after saying the affirmation and shake the energy off. Release it out of a door or window. Sit in a quiet and comfortable place to prepare for your meditation.
Allow the binary tones to play or someone can play a singing bowl during the meditation.

Release Meditation

Sit quietly in a comfortable position.
Breathe out through your mouth and in through the nose.
Relax yourself and focus on your breath.
Allow your mind to be quiet from mental chatter.
Continue to breathe deeply and visualize yourself sitting by the ocean. It is a beautiful warm day. You can feel the sun over your head and the warm sand beneath you.
You can hear the waves crashing and there is a light breeze blowing around you.
You can feel a light mist of water as the wind blows it gently around you.
The water is cooling and calming to your spirit.
Continue to breath and feel the energy of the ocean.
It is purifying and healing. It has a peaceful and calming energy.
Visualize a blue light coming from the ocean.
See the blue light energy moving around you, swirling around you, surrounding you with the blue light energy. Breathe in the blue light energy. Feel in moving into your head.
Allow the blue light energy to clear away all negative thoughts and memories.

*The blue light energy will clear away all sadness, fear and doubts.
It will clear away negative thinking pattern and confusion.
Allow the blue light energy to balance your masculine and feminine parts of your brain.
Feel your head becoming lighter with every breath you take.
Breath out all negative thoughts and memories from your mind.
Let them go and may they be turned into something beautiful.
Breath in deeply and visualize the blue light energy moving into your heart.
It's bringing the energy of peace, love and harmony.
The blue light is swirling through your heart clearing away all negative emotions. It will clear away all hurt, pain, jealousy, envy and anything that makes your heart heavy.
Breathe in the energy of peace and love and breathe out anything that blocks your peace.
Release all heaviness from your heart and mind with each breath.
Allow the blue light energy to make you feel lighter and lighter.
See it moving within you from your head to your toes.
Breath out anything that blocks your peace.
See yourself moving closer to the ocean.
Feel the water at your feet and walk in.
Allow the ocean water to clear your body and your aura.
Splash the water on your head and all over your body.
Release the negativity to the ocean and let yourself be cleansed.
Continue to breathe deeply and feel the clearing of your spirit
Give thanks for the clearing and healing that is happening.
Allow the energy of peace and harmony to fill your head, heart and body.*

Be one with yourself and with the energy of peace.
Allow this energy to flow through you as long as you need it to.
Breath deeply and bring yourself back to your sacred space.
Allow the peaceful energy to stay with you as you bring yourself back to your body.
Feel yourself and become aware of your body.
Take a few more deep breaths and when you are ready you can open your eyes.
Sit and relax as long as you need to.

14. After the meditation, take a few minutes to ground yourself. You can hold a black stone for grounding if you feel light headed after the meditation.

CLOSING:

- Say a prayer of gratitude after the ritual and know that it is done and working on your behalf.

- You can write in your journal or just sit and relax after completing the ritual.

- Make sure to smudge with incense to release any negative energy in your space. You can also open a door or window to allow the energy to flow out of your space while smudging.

- You can allow the candle to burn out completely. Take the altar down when the candle has burned completely.

Heart Healing Ritual

The heart healing ritual is meant to help those who have heavy or cold hearts. We are meant to have feelings so that we can resolve our troubles or issues however we are not meant to stay in our feelings for long periods of time. When we get angry, upset, sad, jealous or have other negative emotions in our hearts, it makes our hearts heavy or blocked.

When our hearts are blocked, we think, speak and act out of our feelings rather that our higher self. When we move or act out of anger or sadness we do not make the best choices for ourselves and our loved ones.

We have to take time to release the years of emotions that we carry so that our hearts can be light and we can be at peace. Once we are at peace we can learn to control our emotions, words and actions and live with more balance and peace.

We have to learn to forgive ourselves and others so our hearts can truly be light. Once we express our emotions and forgive we can let go and live without baggage the past haunting us.

This ritual was created to assist ones with this healing process. It is meant to help you face and resolve the blockages in your heart so you can live your best life in the present and the future.

This ritual can be done as an individual or with a group. It should be performed on Monday, Thursday, Friday or Sunday. Wear pink or green for best results with this ritual.

ITEMS NEEDED:

◊ Rose quartz stones
◊ Pink and/or red roses
◊ Rose, jasmine or lavender essential oils & incense
◊ Rose water
◊ Pink candle
◊ Singing bowl
◊ tissue paper (optional)
◊ White, green or pink cloth for the altar.

When doing healing work with the heart, rose quartz is very helpful. Get five to ten rose quartz stones so you can create a powerful crystal grid.

THE RITUAL:

1. Start with smudging the participants and the space.

2. Light your candle and set your intentions.

3. Pour libation and invoke the energy of the Love Goddesses and your Spirit Guides. You can do this by saying their names and asking them to come and be present for the ritual. You can ask them to assist with bringing love and peace to those who are present. Pray for protection from all negativity.

4. Make a crystal grid with the rose and clear quartz stones. Arrange the crystals in a shape like a heart, circle or other shape Add the stones in a way that looks pretty to you. Let your spirit guide.

5. Put the flowers in the middle of the heart or circle in a vase or on the floor around the participants. Flower petals are good for laying on the floor around the participants.

6. Light rose, jasmine or other floral incense.

7. Give each participant a rose quartz to hold in their hand for the ritual.

8. Next talk a little about the heart to get everyone in tune with the energy of the heart ritual.

The heart is a muscle that is meant to be used for more than moving blood through our bodies. It has to be stretched and exercised with love and experiences just like every other muscle. Our experiences are meant to help us learn lessons and to learn to love ourselves and everything around us.

The heart is the midpoint of the body. It is the place of transformation between the lower and higher self. It is through our lessons of love that we are meant to learn to defeat our lower selves and become elevated enough to live from our higher selves, which means living with unconditional love.

When our hearts are heavy we cannot make that shift and we can get stuck in our lower selves for the rest of our lives. We are not meant to live like that. We are meant to learn to make the right decisions despite adversity and live from our higher selves to live with love, harmony, peace, honesty and good character. That is being God-like and being on the path of enlightenment and immortality.

9. Ask everyone to stand up to stretch. Do movements that invoke movement of the heart (for example bringing your arms together in front of you and then swing them to the back over a few times). Rotate the shoulder and shake your chest to help shake up the stagnant energy in your body. Shake your body, especially the chest and heart to get prepared for the work ahead.

10. Sit down in a circle around the crystal grid for discussion. Ask everyone to speak out about what is making their hearts heavy.

* Prior to the discussion, make sure to declare the room a safe space so that anything that is said will not be repeated outside of the circle. Allow participants to share and speak freely about their experiences. All participants should offer encouraging words after each person speaks. Have tissue available because tears may start to flow.

11. While each individual is speaking, perform sound therapy by playing a singing bowl or other instrument on each individual to assist them in releasing the blockages in their hearts. You may spend five to fifteen minutes on each person.

12. Ask everyone to sit down in a comfortable place for the

guided meditation. They can continue to hold their rose quartz in their hand and put their hands on their hearts. It is best for everyone to lay down if possible. Laying down on a yoga mat is excellent for relaxing and being open to receive the healing energy.

Have someone read the meditation or use our recording..

HEART HEALING MEDITATION

If possible play the singing bowl during the meditation.
Breath deeply and relax (repeat this several time)
Just relax yourself and envision yourself sitting in a field of beautiful flowers.
There are butterflies dancing around you.
There are hummingbirds and birds singing over your head.
The sun is shining over your head and you feel a gentle breeze blowing the fragrance of flowers all around you.
Breath deeply and feel the connection with nature around you.
You are in a safe space, a healing space.
Feel your heart beat and your heart.
Feel the energy in your heart and become aware of your feelings.
Know that you have the ability to breath out all negativity from your heart.
Take deep, slow breaths to clear the energy in your heart.
Breathe in the energy of the flowers around you.
The flowers carry the energy of peace, joy and love.
Breathe out everything that make your heart heavy.
Breathe out sadness.

Breathe out fear and anger.

Take your time to breathe and release the emotions from your mind, heart and body.

Breathe out fear, disappointment, bitterness.

Breathe out stress, pressure and pain.

Breathe out old memories and experiences.

Breathe deeply and allow your heart to become light.

Feel your heart becoming lighter with every breath you take.

Breathe in healing pink light, energy into your heart.

Pink like the rose quartz.

Allow the pink light energy to bring love and healing light into your heart.

Breathe in peace and love with that pink light energy.

Feel the pink light sending love through your mind, your body and down to your toes.

Allow the pink light to move through your entire body and feel yourself becoming lighter with each breath.

Feel the love energy flowing through you and around you.

Feel the love energy moving to each part of your body.

Feel the love light energy flowing to your organs, glands and blood.

Feel the love energy flowing from the universe into every part of you.

Know that you are loved and adored.

Know that you are divine and healed.

Breathe deeply and let that energy continue to flow through you.

Feel the energy of deep peace and love within your heart and mind.

Allow the peace and love vibration to continue to flow within and

around you knowing that you can come back to this place at any time.
Now breathe deeply and bring yourself back to your body and this sacred space.
Take another deep breath and open our eyes in five.... four... three... two ... one.
Open your eyes and return to normal breathing.
Sit and relax as long as you need to.

13. When you feel the participants are pass around the rose or lavender essential oil. Ask them to anoint their forehead and heart with the oil. let them repeat the affirmations three or more times.

14. As they anoint themselves they can repeat the Heart Healing Affirmations

Heart Healing Affirmations

I love myself.
I love every part of me.
I am love and accept myself the way that I am.
I love my body, organs and glands.
I love my hair, my nose and my eyes.
I am in love with myself.
I love myself and I forgive myself for my mistakes.
I love myself enough to be the best version of myself.
I love myself so much that I make the best decisions for myself.

My heart is open to receive divine, unconditional love.
I am loved divinely and I give love in a divine way.
Pure, unconditional love lives and moves through me.
I think, speak and act with love.
I am compassionate with myself and others.
I am compassionate and loving to the earth.
I am compassionate and loving to the Ancestors.
My Heart is as light as a feather.
From this day forward.
So be it and so it is!

(Repeat these affirmations as needed)

CLOSING:

- Use two or three flowers per person to clear everyone's aura by sweeping the flowers down the front and back of their bodies. Release the flowers outside after using them.
- Take a moment to share a prayer of gratitude to the Spirit Guides for their assistance.
- Smudge everyone or allow them to sprinkle themselves with a spiritual bath.
- Give time for ones to share if they like.
- Take the altar down when the candles have burned completely.
- Take the Heart Healing Spiritual bath after doing the ritual, before bedtime is best.

Heart Healing Spiritual Bath

ITEMS NEEDED:
- Rose quartz
- Pink & white flower petals
- Rose (or another floral essential oil)
- Rose water
- Sea salt
- 1 tablespoon of honey
- Dash of cinnamon

- Add the items to a metal, glass or wood bowl (do not use a plastic bowl). As you add the items think of love and forgiveness and put your intentions into the bath.
- Only add the flower petals, no stems, and tear the petals into little pieces while you focus on love and healing your heart.
- Add purified water to the bowl and say a prayer or say the affirmations as you mix everything together.
- Use this to soak in or pour it over yourself using a small bowl or cup after a shower.

This bath can be taken for five days after the ritual or as needed.

Release from Sexual trauma Ritual

Sexual Trauma is a plague in our community that affects men, women and children. Sexual trauma can include, rape, molestation, abuse, sodomy, mishandling and more. Some forms of sexual trauma were inflicted as a means of oppression and control of one over another. Sexual trauma occurs when one is left feeling violated or hurt during or after a sexual encounter. Often it happens without the consent of the victim. This is the root of the trauma. One can be left feeling powerless, unprotected, unloved and a variety of other emotions as a result of sexual trauma that have to be healed or brought into balance within.

Some who have been sexually abused do not speak about their abuse because they were told to keep it a secret. Keeping such a secret can lead to one becoming distant or quiet in relationships. There is healing that should be done to release the emotions and the energy from sexual trauma. This is not something that can be healed overnight and counseling can be helpful for someone to move forward in their life without carrying the baggage of pain and other emotions that occur as a result of sexual abuse.

This ritual can be helpful for one to begin the process of healing themselves so they can have better self-esteem and better relationships with themselves and others This is only part of the work that needs to be done for complete healing and balance.

This ritual can be performed in a group or alone. It is helpful to wear white or other light colors when doing this particular ritual. The best days to perform the ritual are Sunday, Monday, or Friday.

ITEMS NEEDED:

- White candle
- Pen and paper
- Bowl of water
- Clear quartz
- Black crystal (tourmaline, jet, shungite, onyx, obsidian)
- Frankincense and myrrh incense
- Dance music
- Charcoal & burning pot
- Cloth for altar (purple, blue or white)

THE RITUAL:

1. Smudge everyone and the space with frankincense & myrrh.

2. Light the candle and state your intentions for the ritual.

3. Pour libations (by pouring water on the ground or in a plant) and call on your Benevolent Ancestors, Spirit Guides, Angels, Deities and/or The Great Mothers by saying their names. Ask them to come and be present to assist with the healing ritual. Ask that they keep all negativity away.

4. Take a moment to speak about sexual abuse.

Sexual trauma is a violation of one's personal space and body through sexual or intimate contact. It can be considered as an energy or entity that is passed from one to another through sexual contact. Sexual abuse is usually used as a means of control by ones with power or those who have less power. Children, boys and girls, women as well as elders are victims of abuse. The strong prey on those who are less strong.

Because sexual abuse affects in our lower self, near our reproductive organs, this is the area we want to focus on clearing spiritually. Sexual abuse also affects ones mind (thoughts) and their hearts or emotions. So these are the aspects of the self that we focus on during this ritual. Allow others to share their thoughts.

5, After the discussion take a moment to dance, turn on some positive and upbeat music and shake your hips and your body.

Get everyone up and moving and focus on waist winding and hip movements. This will help to shift the stagnant energy in your lower self.

6, After dancing take a moment to allow everyone to share about their personal experience. Encourage everyone to share any details you feel comfortable with sharing as well as how you feel now about your experience. Allow others to do the same.

If the emotions get to strong cry or yell (if possible) and let it out as necessary. Give each person an opportunity to express their feelings. expressing feelings and sharing your story is a part of the healing process. In my twenty years of experience as a healer I have found that when people are able to speak about a hurtful situation without becoming emotional, they have reached a level of healing that allows them to feel more balanced and at peace within. So you want to take about your experiences in a healthy way with those that can support, care and love you through it until you begin to find peace within.

7. After the sharing session, write down the name of the person (or persons) that violated you on a sheet of paper. When finished writing, tear the paper up into small pieces while releasing the energy and emotions you have been holding.

8. Take the little pieces of paper and put them in the bowl of water. The water will neutralize and dissolve the energy away. Put the bowel of water next to your candle.

9. Say these affirmations after you tear your paper and use them later as needed to help you reprogram yourself.

HEALING FROM SEXUAL ABUSE AFFIRMATIONS

My past no longer has power over me.
I am in control of myself and my divine power.
I release the past experiences that do not serve my highest good.
I release all negative ties and bonds to my abuser(s).

I release negative emotions that hold me down.
I have overcome my pain and my past challenges.
I am in a sweet, new cycle of my life.
I love myself completely.
I deserve to be loved fully and unconditionally.
I deserve to always be treated with compassion and respect.
I am worthy of great and divine relationships.
I am whole and I feel great.

10. After saying the affirmations, use the black stone and rub it all over your body starting at your head. Visualize the stone absorbing any emotions, memories or other negativity that does not serve you. Allow it to absorb all negative energy from your auric field. Make sure to rub it around your head, under your arms, between your legs and under your feet. Place the stone in a plant or window seal once complete to recharge it.

11. Next prepare for your meditation.

12. You can create a crystal grid with the black stones around you. Lay down and put a stone on each side of your head, around the heart area, around your sexual organs and at your feet.
You can also put stones directly on your heart and lower body (reproductive organs).

13. Turn on binary tones for self-love and releasing negativity.

Healing From Sexual Abuse Meditation

Lay down in a comfortable position.

Take a few deep breaths and relax.

Breathe in through your nose and expand your abdomen.

Breathe out through your mouth and squeeze your belly and squeeze your lower muscles to push all of the air out of you.

Do this three times.

Then reverse your breath. Breath in and squeeze your belly and breathe out while expanding your belly.

Do this three time to clear and restart your energy.

Next return to normal breathing.

Relax yourself with each breath.

Allow your body to sink into the floor and just relax.

Close your eyes and visualize yourself at the age of your first violation.

See yourself having fun, smiling and laughing.

Go to your inner child, and give her a hug.

Tell her that she is safe and all is well.

Tell her that no one will hurt her ever again.

Apologize to yourself and forgive yourself.

Send loving energy to your inner child and to every part of you.

See your inner child being surrounded by ones that you love.

Allow yourself to feel safe and protected among these loved ones.

Allow yourself to be filled and surrounded by healing love energy.

Allow yourself to laugh to be happy and to be at peace during this time in your life.

Breathe in the energy of peace and love.

Breathe out anything that blocks your peace of mind.

See yourself loving yourself and having good relationships with others.

Know that you are loved and divinely protected.

You are fine and all is well.

You will never be hurt like that again.

You will never be around ones who will hurt you.

You are strong and you have overcome your challenges.

You are a different person.

Your inner child is whole and happy.

All is well.

Give thanks and praises.

So be it and so it is.

Allow this feeling of peace and happiness to stay with you and know that you can return to this place at any time.

Take a deep breath and return now back to this sacred space.

When you are ready you can open your eyes.

Sit and relax as long as you need to.

Take a few minutes to let everyone return to their bodies.

14. Tell everyone to take the bowl of water and flush it down the toilet. As the paper goes down the drain, know that the energy is being cleared away.

CLOSING:

◊ Say a prayer of gratitude to the Ancestors and Spirit Guides for their energy and participation.

◊ Allow the candle to burn out completely.

◊ Take the spiritual bath for three to five days after the ritual.

◊ Repeat the affirmations for the next twenty one days and beyond if you like.

◊ Start the first Spiritual bath after the ritual before you go to bed.

◊ Allow the altar to stay up for two to three months or as long as you feel like you need it.

HEALING FROM SEXUAL TRAUMA AFFIRMATIONS

My experiences made me the divine being that I am.

I am safe and protected at all times.

I no longer hold on to hurt, harm and pain from my past.

I release blockages from my past.

I release the negative energy of others.

I do not let anyone abuse or violate me.

I attract ones who will love and honor me.

I attract peaceful and healthy relationships.

I adore myself and I attract those who adore me.

I attract relationships that build, heal and encourage me to be the best version of myself.

I deserve the best of everything.

My life is perfect for me.

Healing From Sexual Trauma Spiritual Bath

Items Needed:

- Black crystal
- Sea salt or Epsom salt
- Apple cider vinegar
- Baking soda
- Peroxide
- Florida water
- One lemon
- White or yellow flowers
- Frankincense oil

Add the items to a metal, glass or wood bowl (don't use plastic). As you add the items focus on self-love and forgiveness and put your intentions into the bath. Only add the flower petals, no stems, and tear the petals into little pieces while you focus on a new cycle of loving yourself and healing your heart.

Add purified water to the bowl and say a prayer or say the affirmations as you mix everything together. Allow the bath to sit for thirty minutes or more before you use it. Use this to soak in or pour it over yourself after a shower.

Say the affirmations or your own prayer as you take the bath. This bath should be taken for three to five consecutive days after the ritual. It can be used weekly after that. It will help to clear the energy of others from your aura and spiritual bodies.

Womb Healing Ritual

Women have given birth to humanity. As a women you carry sacred energy in your womb that allows you to carry and birth to another human, which is incredible. The wombs of women are the center of creation, power and creativity. You have the ability to create whatever you can conceive in your mind with the energy that you carry in your womb. You receive energy, love, power, pleasure and sometimes pain within your womb.

So you also have a tendency to also hold negative emotions in your womb. This can contribute to cysts, fibroids and other womb dis-ease. When you are intimate and have sexual intercourse with someone you exchange DNA and spiritual energy. Your womb will carry the energy of those who you allow to enter this sacred chamber. Here are some things to consider:

- If you have a toxic partner you will have a toxic womb.
- If you have had many sexual partners (more than one new person per year).
- If you have used sex toys or used other unnatural (plastic) items in your womb it can be harmful and cause toxicity.
- If you use birth control for over five years it can cause stagnant energy within your womb.
- If you have had a violent or harmful breakup or had sexual abuse in any form your womb may be stagnant and toxic.

This ritual will assist in breaking any ties or bonds from past relationships that do not serve you. It will assist you in clearing negative emotions and energy from your womb.

Wear white, pink or blue when you perform this ritual.

Good days for this ritual are Sunday, Monday and Friday.

ITEMS NEEDED:
- Green candle for healing
- White candle for purification
- Pink candle for love
- 3 rose quartz crystals
- 2 clear quartz crystals
- 5 or more blue crystals (lapis lazuli, sodalite, turquoise, moonstone)
- Frankincense resin
- Rose petals
- Lavender flowers
- Charcoal
- Metal pot or bowl to burn charcoal

THE RITUAL:

1. Create an altar with the items in your bedroom. Use a white, green or pink cloth as a base. Add a picture of yourself and arrange the crystals around the picture in a beautiful way. Add things like flowers, oils, perfume, mirrors, other items that make you feel good about healing your womb.

2. Light the white candle first and speak your intentions.

3. Light the charcoal and burn the frankincense.

4. Say a prayer from your heart asking for your womb to be cleared of negative energy and the energy of others.

5. Lay down and meditate with the blue crystals on your womb and the clear and rose quartz crystals around you.

6. Visualize the blue stones absorbing and balancing the energy in your womb. Breathe in the energy of peace. Breathe with your womb (kegels) and push out the energy that you want to release with your breath.

7. Continue to relax and lay down for your meditation.

8. Put your hands in the shape of a pyramid and put them over your reproductive organs.

WOMB HEALING MEDITATION

Breathe deeply and focus on your breath. (repeat this 3 times)
Breathe with your lower muscles as well. (kegel exercise)
Contract them as you breathe out and release them as you breathe in.
Focus on releasing all negativity as you breathe out.
Continue to breathe slowly and deeply.
Relax yourself more and more with each breath.
Visualize yourself out in a forest.
There is life and energy all around you.
The birds are singing, butterflies are flying.

*The sun is shining brightly and there is a gentle breeze blowing.
You can hear the sound of water flowing off in the distance.
You feel a connection with the earth and the life around you.
It is a peaceful space, full of life and divine energy.
There are flowers blooming around you and the trees are full of fruits and flowers as well.
Allow yourself to feel the beauty of the earth.
Tune in to the abundance of the earth.
See yourself walking closer to the water and there is a beautiful waterfall in front of you.
The water is flowing and it looks so inviting.
It is drawing you, calling you closer.
You can feeling the power and the energy of the water.
You can feel a sprinkle of water on your arms and face as you get closer.
This is a magical healing waterfall that will wash away your pain and sadness.
The magical healing waters will cleanse your physical, emotional, mental and spiritual bodies.
You jump into the crystal clear waters and stand under the falls.
You can feel the water clearing away negativity.
Feel the magical waters flowing into your womb clearing away old, toxic energy.
Each drop of water that touches you is cleansing you in all ways.
Allow the water to clear your sadness and negative emotions
Allow the water to clear your memory, your womb and your heart.*

Stand there as long as you need to, until you feel clear and light.

Take the time to clear and purify yourself in the Magical healing waterfalls.

When you are ready come out of the water and lay on the grass.

Allow the sun to dry you and charge your energy with pure light and divine love.

Let the love energy from the water and the sun fill your body from head to toe.

Let the love energy fill your heart and your mind.

Feel the connection with the earth and with the Divine.

Remember this feeling and stay in it as long as you need to.

Know that you can return to this place of peace at any time.

Take a deep breath and return now to your body and to your own sacred space.

Take another deep breath and when you are ready you can open your eyes.

Take some time to return to yourself.

Relax as long as you need to.

CLOSING:

- Say a prayer of gratitude to the Spirit Guides, Ancestors and Great Mothers for their assistance.

- Allow the white candle to burn out completely and when it is finished light the pink candle. Allow the pink candle to burn out completely as well.

- Take the spiritual bath to clear any residual energy that needs to be released. Focus on purification and healing when you prepare the bath. It is good to take a spiritual bath to clear your aura and the spiritual energy of your womb to release lingering emotions and the energy of those which you are no longer connected to.

- Say these affirmations daily for fourteen days or use them later when you feel like you need strength.
- Take the spiritual bath after you perform the ritual before you go to bed.
- go to the altar on Mondays or Fridays and light a candle to keep the energy flowing for up to three months after you perform the ritual.

AFFIRMATIONS FOR WOMB HEALING

I release the negative emotions that block my womb.

I release karmic and spiritual ties from my womb.

I release the energy of others from my womb.

I release sickness and disease from my womb.

I allow healing energy to rejuvenate my womb.

I allow divine healing in my heart, my spirit and my soul.

I am pure in mind, body and spirit.

My womb is more pure now than ever before.

My womb is light and perfectly healthy.

I am thankful.

Womb Healing Spiritual bath

This bath is specifically for womb healing and clearing. You can take it every Monday for seven weeks or as often as you like.

ITEMS NEEDED:

- White carnation flowers
- Red clover herb
- Red raspberry
- Hyssop
- White sage
- Frankincense oil or rose oil
- Sea salt
- Rose water
- Honey
- 3 limes

Cut the limes into wedges and mix them with the other items in a large bowl.

Crush the leaves and flowers with your hands and pray for your womb healing as you do so.

After two or three minutes add pure filter spring water to the bowl and mix with your hands.

Ask your Ancestors and Spirit Guides to help you heal and release that which is not good for you.

Let the bath sit for an hour or more, then add to a warm tub of water and sit in the bath for 20 to 30 minutes.

Pray for your healing and visualize your womb becoming lighter and more at peace while you are in the bath.

Release any sickness, sadness or worries into the water and claim your healing by speaking the words aloud.

Speak from your heart about what you want to release and be specific (release people, emotions and memories for example) and when you are finished, you can rinse yourself off with cold water in the shower to free yourself from any remnants of energy.

After the bath dress in light colors. Avoid TV, radio, social media and other distractions.

Stay in a place of peace and balance.

It is best to do this bath right before you go to bed.

Men's Healing Ritual

Men need healing too. Men are sometime slow to realize they need to slow down to heal themselves. Many men have had difficulties during childhood from neglect to abuse and they have not gotten counseling or help with resolving some of the emotions that they have. 'they may also need to heal from relationships with their parents, siblings, partners and so on.

Men are usually taught to hold their emotion in and be strong when they are young and by the time they reach their twenties they may be full of mixed emotions that have not been processed or resolved. This can lead to dysfunctional behavior, negative thinking habits, addictive behavior, oversexualization and other toxic masculine behavior patterns.

As a man you have to heal from toxic relationships, heartbreak and anger from living in a society of fear, oppression and racism. You can sometimes lack self esteem or can be overly confident and aggressive as a result of not healing from your relationships.

There are also issues of oversexualization of men. You have aggressive energy that must be channeled in a positive way for you to stay healthy and balanced. This energy can be channeled through sports, exercise, music, dance, or other physical activity. If these things are not available the energy is used sexually through masturbation or excessive intercourse. Sexual release can become an imbalanced habit that some men need to bring into balance to have a better quality of life.

Here are some things to consider:

- If you have been in a series of relationships you may need to stop and take time to heal yourself.
- If you don't have a good relationship with your parents or your children, you may need to heal yourself.
- If you don't have good relationships with women or men, you may need to do some healing.
- If you have several sexual partners at the same time but they don't know about each other, making your life miserable, you may need to stop and do some healing for yourself.
- If you have a hard time handling your responsibilities, you may need to do some healing.

This ritual is create to help men release negative energy and reconnect with their divine masculine power.

This is a two part ritual, the first part should be done outside in the woods. The other part can be done at your home.

This ritual can be done alone or in a group.

Good days for this ritual are Tuesday, Thursday, Saturday or Sunday. These are days with a masculine influence.

Wear white, blue ore green when you perform the ritual for best results.

Items Needed:

- Drum
- White candle (for purification)
- Green candle (for healing and strength)
- Benzoin or palo santo incense
- Sandalwood oil
- Tobacco
- Gin or clear rum
- Sweets or fruits (for offering)
- Coins
- White or green cloth for the altar
- Charcoal and a burning pot for incense

The Ritual:

The first part of this ritual should be done outside in a wooded area. Choose an area that is quiet and private. This ritual can be done alone or in a group.

1. Take the drum and play a slow steady rhythm as you walk into the woods. Find a clearing with a large old tree to stop for the ritual.

2. Make offerings to the largest and oldest tree by setting the items at the base of the tree and saying a prayer of gratitude to the energy of the tree, the Earth and the energy around you.

The offerings are a token to the masculine energy of the trees and the earth. When you leave offerings it represents you giving back for all that you have been given.

3. Take time to ask for forgiveness for anything that you have done wrong at this time as well. Ask for forgiveness for hurting yourself and others. Be specific with your words and say it like you mean it out loud.

4. After making offerings, take a moment to hug or touch the tree with both hands. Ask the tree to absorb any negative energy that should be taken off of you. Ask to be cleared of the energy of others and all that does not serve your highest good.

5. Gather some of the tree bark, leaves, pine cones or needles and roots with you to use for your spiritual bath. Do not get things that look dead or full of insects.

6. Find some tree branches with leaves (shiny leaves) in the woods around you. Pick a tree branch and use it to clear your aura. Start at your head and work down the body in a sweeping motion with the tree branch to clear away any sticky or stagnant negative energy. When you are finished with the branches throw them far away from you.

7. Pick a spot to sit and meditate as long as you need to. Reflect on your feelings and emotions. Think about the things that you need to heal from. Think about the things that make you feel sad, angry and uncomfortable and allow yourself some time to find peace with those things. Forgive yourself and others for any pain you may be holding. Breathe slowly and deeply and release stress, fear, anger and any other negative emotions you need to let go of through your breath.

8. If you need to cry, holler, laugh, scream or shake the energy and emotions off of you. Take this opportunity to leave your worries and stress in nature and let it be absorbed and transformed into something beautiful.

9. When you feel lighter chant AMEN RA (or call any name of the CREATOR) five or more times before you leave. Tap into the power of the Divine and all of nature.

10. Leave the offerings where they are, make sure to take any trash or plastic with you. When you walk away don't look back.

11. When you get home create an Altar of Divine Masculine Power. Use a cloth of your choice or none at all. Get pictures of men that you admire, they can be in your family or not. If you don't have pictures you can write a list of their names. You can

add men who are living, ancestors, deities, angels or other men that you feel have Divine Masculine energy.

12. Light your incense while you are building the Altar.

13. Light your white and green candles and arrange them on the altar in a way that feels special to you.

14. Add the crystals to the altar. Add other items that represent masculine energy, for example a truck, a piece of gold or roots from a tree. Arrange the items in a way that feels good to you. Be sure to wash all items off first before placing them on the altar.

15. When you finish the altar sit and play your drum again (you can also play drum music from YouTube). Pour a libation and say the names of the men that you have on your list. Pray for their spirits to be at peace then ask them to assist you in your healing process. Ask them to work with you and to guide you. Speak from your heart and say what you feel you need to say.

16. You can also write down a list of things goals to add to your altar. It can be six month, one year, three or five year goals. Writing your goals helps you to remember what you need to work on.

17. When you are finished writing prepare for your meditation

Men's Healing Meditation

Sit in a quiet and comfortable position.

Relax and breathe deeply.

In through the mouth and out through the nose.

Relax more and more with each breath.

Return to normal breathing.

Focus on your heartbeat.

Allow yourself to become lighter and lighter as you relax.

Visualize yourself outside in a beautiful field.

The sun is shining brightly over your head and there is a gentle breeze blowing to keep you cool.

You can hear the birds singing and it is a beautiful day.

Connect with the energy of the sun and feel the energy of the sun moving through you.

Breathe in the energy of the sun and allow it to fill your body.

As you breath in more sunlight energy notice that you begin to feel the light energy moving in your head.

It is clearing away old thinking patterns and habits that do not serve you.

As you breath in more sunlight energy you can feel it moving through your throat clearing away negative words you have said to yourself and others.

When you breath again you feel the sunlight energy moving into your heart, clearing away pain and blockages in your heart..

As you breathe in sunlight energy breathe out all blockages and stagnant energy in your body.

The sunlight energy continues to flow through you bringing peace, strength, courage, and divine masculine energy.

You can feel it moving from your head to your toes.

It is bringing healing to your mind, body and spirit.

It is filling you with the energy of the Divine Creator, pure love.

and power while activating your own creative power.

Allow the sunlight energy to continue to flow through you rejuvenating, renewing and restoring the cells in your body.

Feel the connection that you have with the sun.

Feel the connection that you have with the elements.

Feel the connection you have with the universe.

Continue to breathe deeply and allow the energy to continue to flow as long as it needs to.

When you are ready take another deep breath.

See yourself returning to your body and to your space.

Breathe deeply and open your eyes in five... four... three... two... one.

Return to normal breathing.

Just sit and relax as long as you need to.

CLOSING:

- Say a prayer of gratitude and give thanks to the energy of the men that you called on for the ritual.

- Allow the candles to continue to burn until they burn out completely.

- Go to the altar a few times a week, (Tuesday, Thursday, Saturday or Sunday are days with a masculine influence) and light a candle or just sit and meditate.

- Take the recommended Men's Healing Spiritual Bat each Sunday for 9 weeks if possible.

- Write a commitment statement to yourself and your family stating what you will do as you step into a more whole and balanced cycle of your life. Say this commitment statement daily or as you choose to help you reaffirm the principles that you want to live by in your life.

- Take time to share with other men who are younger and older than you. The time that we share and give to others can be very healing and helpful for your heart and emotions.

- Be loving to yourself and others in the way you speak, think and act.

- Say the affirmations to raise your vibration and raise your consciousness daily or use your own as you choose.

MEN'S HEALING AFFIRMATIONS

I am Strong Man

I am powerful.

I will not use my power to abuse anyone.

I will not let others misuse or abuse me.

I honor my manhood.

I am a warrior of peace, protection & upliftment.

I am accountable for any and all of my errors and I am also willing to correct them.

I will protect myself and all women in my life to my greatest ability.

I do not determine my manhood based on ego nor by the belittlement of others.

I determine my manhood by principles of righteous empowerment.

I will take responsibility for the youth around me so they can become better men and women.

I am willing to heal myself.

I love myself.

All is well and I am grateful.

Men's Healing Spiritual Bath

Items Needed:

- Tree bark
- Pine cones or needles
- Sandalwood oil
- Rosemary
- Gin or clear rum
- Sea or Epsom salt
- Baking soda
- Peroxide
- Sage
- Clear quartz crystal

Add the items to a metal, glass or wood bowl (do not use a plastic bowl).

As you add the items, think of healing, releasing, restoring and renewal and put your intentions into the bath.

You can wash off the bark and break it into small pieces with the other items.

Add purified water to the bowl and say a prayer or say the affirmations as you mix everything together.

Use this to soak in or pour it over yourself after a shower.

Say the affirmations or your own words as you take the bath.

This bath should be taken once a week for three months or more. It will help to clear away the energy of others from your aura and spiritual bodies and help with strength, motivation and clarity.

Relationship Elevation Ritual

Our first relationship is the relationship we have with ourselves. Other relationships reflect the way we feel about ourselves. We learn to relate and communicate with others first at home when we are children. Our relationship with our Mothers will determine how we love and communicate with others.

Mother is the first teacher and the way she talks to us and loves us is how we learn to love and communicate with others. If that relationship with mother is strained, abusive, neglectful or absent during childhood it can lead one to become withdrawn, mistrustful, unstable, dishonest, and other to have other negative traits. The childhood habits will affect your other relationships until healing occurs to change and correct the negative habits and thinking patterns. It takes time, months or years to make these changes so be patient with yourself and others during this process.

Holding grudges, not speaking to each other, arguing and fighting are not good habits to have in relationships. We have to learn how to communicate to resolve our issues. Sometimes it is helpful to ask Divine Spirit to intervene and assist to bring balance to relationships.

This ritual can be helpful to heal any relationship whether it is parent to child, sibling issues or issues between intimate partners.

Before you begin the work write a letter or letters to express your feelings to those you want to have better relationships with. Clearly state what you feel the issues are, then write about what your desires for the relationship are. Remember love is the greatest healer of all, so be loving with your words in your letters. Write in a language that you would not mind reading aloud. Take your time and say all that you need to say. This letter will be added to your healing altar. If you want to read it to the one you wrote to that is fine but not necessary.

For this ritual, choose a day with feminine energy such as Monday or Friday. Dress in yellow, white or green when your perform this ritual.

ITEMS NEEDED:

- Green seven day candle
- Tea light candles
- Green aventurine or rose quartz crystal
- Crystal heart of symbol of love
- Honey
- Cinnamon
- Sweets (candy, fruit, pie, cake, etc..)
- Green or white cloth for the altar

THE RITUAL:

1. Create your healing altar in a space where you will see it often. Use a green cloth or choose one of your favorite colors. Use a small table and add pictures (if possible) of those who you want to have better relationships with, for example add a picture of you and your mate or just a picture of your mother.

2. You will want to say the names your righteous Ancestors and Spirit Guides to work with you. Ask for protection and you can also call on the CREATOR, angel or Great Mothers for assistance.

3. Construct the altar with the picture in the middle and the crystals around the picture. Add a bowl of honey and taste a bit.

4. Light your incense and then your green candle. State your intentions for the ritual while you light the candle.

5. Read your letter aloud and then place it under the candle when you are finished.

6. Sit in a comfortable place and prepare for your meditation.

RELATIONSHIP ELEVATION MEDITATION

Breathe deeply and relax.

Breath in through your nose and out through your mouth.

Breath in for four counts.

Hold for four counts then breath out for four counts.

Repeat four count breathing until you relax completely.

Visualize yourself sitting at the top of a mountain.

See yourself sitting with the person that you want to have a better relationship with.

Greet them with smiles and hugs.

Apologize to their spirit and ask them to forgive you for anything that you did to offend or hurt them.

Visualize them doing the same and see you smiling at each other.

Visualize you both going out to beautiful places, enjoying each other and creating new happy memories.

See yourself laughing and happy with this person as you move through the future.

Envision the relationship going exactly the way you want it to.

Allow yourself to bask in that energy of joy and peace as long as you need to.

Continue to hold that vision and that feeling as you take a deep breath.

When you are ready return back to your body and your sacred space.

Take a deep breath and give thanks for the healing that has occurred.

Take another deep breath and when you are ready you can open your eyes.

Sit and relax as long as you need to.

7. Once complete know that the energy will be working for you as you go through your days. You may begin to notice changes happening gradually. Always remember to keep your heart and

the communication open. Be kind and loving when you deal with others, treat others the way you want to be treated. You can light a tea light candle on the altar once a week until you feel like the work is complete.

CLOSING:

- Say a prayer of gratitude to those who came to assist with the ritual.
- Allow the energy to work as it is meant to.
- Allow the candle to burn out completely.
- Keep the altar up. Light a candle at the altar and say a short prayer there at least once a week for three to six months.
- Take a spiritual bath to open the way for the healing to occur.
- Remember that it is best to do this with someone in your family or are tied to in some way. This is not meant to help you get into a relationship with someone against their will.
- Read the letter you wrote when the relationship feels strained or troubled.
- Say the affirmations to put your desires and intentions out into the universe.

Relationship Elevation Affirmations

My relationship with myself is outstanding.

I communicate with myself and others with truth, love, compassion and kindness.

I am thankful for healing and uplifting relationships.

I love and appreciate those who are in my life.

I forgive myself and others for our mistakes.

I forgiven for the hurt that I have caused to others.

I attract supportive and loving relationships.

I honor and respect my relationships.

Relationship Elevation Spiritual Bath

ITEMS NEEDED:
- Jasmine oil
- Rose oil
- Rose water
- River or ocean water
- Purple and white flowers
- Red crystal
- Sea or Epsom salt
- Honey
- 2 lemons (cut into pieces)
- Dash of cayenne pepper

Add the items to a metal, glass or wood bowl (do not use a plastic bowl).

As you add the items, think about love, healing and forgiveness and speak your intentions into the bath.

Only add the flower petals, no stems, and tear the petals into little pieces while you focus on love and healing your heart.

Add purified water to the bowl and say a prayer or say the affirmations as you mix everything together. Let it sit for thirty minutes or more before you use it.

Use this to soak in or pour it over yourself after a shower.

This bath can be taken once a week after the ritual or as needed.

As you take the bath ask to release any blockages that prevent you from having better relationships with yourself and others. Forgive yourself for any mistakes you have made.

Forgive others for things they may have done to hurt or harm you.

Wash away old emotions from your mind and body and be open to having the loving relationships that you desire.

As you leave the bath, imagine that all the old emotions or experiences that you left behind is going down the tub.

Anoint yourself with the jasmine oil on your head and heart.

Wear light colors after the bath. It is best to write in your journal or go to sleep after taking a spiritual bath. Avoid TV, social media and phone conversations that may distract you. Just relax and let the ritual work on you.

FAMILY ELEVATION RITUAL

Families are the foundation of our community. Without strong families we don't have a community at all. It takes strong, whole, healthy individuals to build a strong family. All families have issues or problems, what is important is how you react and handle the problems that come up. The healing work starts with each individual and then moves to those we are connected to.

Blood is thicker than water is an old saying in our community, however that was at a time where there were more people living with boundaries and morals. There have always been things that happen within families that can create division, negative emotions and challenges. These issues can continue to divide and dismantle the family if left unresolved. When secrets are kept it is something that should be discussed and worked out among the family when possible. Sometimes families just don't have information on how to resolve their issues and communicate effectively.

One way that families handled issues in the past was to go to the graveyard, as a family, where "Big Mama" the family matriarch, and the family ancestors were buried. Once their family members would talk it out and have a conversation with the ancestors. Everything was brought out that needed to be addressed and problems were resolved and peace was made before everyone left.

Another way that things were handled in the past was with through using the elders wisdom. Those who had issues would set a time to meet with the older ones in the family (the elders) to share their issues. Then the elders would go to mediate and discuss the situation among themselves. Everything was brought to the table and a decision on how to proceed would be determined and agreed upon among them. The solution will then be shared with the ones seeking help at that time in a formal discussion.

If that is not possible for you to do this ritual may prove to be helpful. It does involve inviting family members to come together to discuss the concerning matter. A talking stick or other item can be used to help keep the discussion smooth.

It is best to perform this ritual on a Monday, Friday or Sunday.

Ask everyone to wear white or a specific color for unity.

ITEMS NEEDED:

* Green ribbon, yarn or string
* Green candle
* Flowers
* Pictures of family members
* Green and purple crystals
* Bowl of water
* Frankincense and myrrh incense
* White or yellow cloth for the altar
* Charcoal and burning pot for incense

THE RITUAL:

1. Create an altar with yellow or white cloth. Add candle, crystals, flowers, a bowl of water and pictures of the family members. Arrange the items on the altar in a way that feels balanced

2.. Call the family to come together in advance. Choose a time that will give you two to three uninterrupted time together. Turn off your cell phones and the television during the ritual time.

3. Ask the family to sit in a circle and discuss the meaning of the gathering. You are coming together to bring harmony to the family, to settle differences, to resolve issues, etc....

4. Before getting started light your incense and candle. State your intentions while you light your candle. Put your crystals around the circle near your family members to help keep the energy positive.

5. Smudge everyone in attendance with the frankincense and myrrh, by moving the burning incense smoke around their bodies. This will help everyone to be in alignment mentally and spiritually for the discussion.

6. Ask the eldest one in attendance say a pray or pour libation to call in the Divine Spirit and the righteous ancestors. Ask everyone to sit in a circle and hold hands while the prayer is being said.

7. Take a few minutes to breath and become in sync with each other. Breathe in through your nose and out through your mouth.

Continue to hold hands while breathing. Then release hands after everyone is more relaxed, after taking about three to five deep breaths.

8. Use a green crystal as a "talking stick" and announce that only the one who holds the green crystal can speak. Give the talking stick to the eldest one in the circle to begin the discussion with questions about what is going on.

9. Take the green string and wrap it around the wrist of the oldest one in attendance. Tie a knot in the string to make a bracelet. Then pass it around the circle to each one so they can do the same. The green string being wrapped around the wrist symbolizes unity and healing for the family. Allow each one to keep their green bracelet on while having the discussion.

10. Allow each one to speak as needed until everyone has had their opportunity. Do your best to speak calmly and without arguing, cursing or name calling. We have to learn how to deal with our issues like mature adults.

11. Seek to find a solution to any problem that comes up during the discussion. Encourage everyone to share what is on their minds and to speak freely. Allow the elder to be the moderator in the discussion to keep things from getting too emotional.

Suggest changes and comprises to assist with the solutions and resolution of the problems.

12. Encourage each one to apologize and to forgive each other. Ask what can be done to avoid this situation from occurring again in the future.

If the discussion becomes overheated and out of control, those who cannot control their words or emotions should leave the circle until they calm down. Others should try to continue to seek resolve. Another meeting can be scheduled if there is little or no progress. Some family members may know how to communicate better than others, however our families should encourage each other to communicate and solve problems within the family. Learning to communicate with love and compassion is an important part of the healing process.

13. When everyone is finished speaking cut the strings of the cord and tell everyone to keep their bracelet on for at least seven days or more, it will help them to remember the discussion and the changes that were suggested.

CLOSING:

* Ask if everyone has learned a lesson from the experience. The elder should be able to point out key lessons for everyone in the family to remember.
* Close the circle and say a prayer of gratitude to the ancestors for their divine guidance and assistance. Have a group hug with everyone in the family. Say a positive chant

* You can sing a favorite family song to close the circle and end on a positive vibration.
* Smudge everyone with the sage or incense and the space before leaving.
* Allow the candle to burn out completely.
* Continue to pray for the healing of the family.
* Say these affirmations before and after the ritual.
* Keep the altar up for seven days or more and light a candle or say affirmations when conflict arises or when you feel the need to do so.

AFFIRMATIONS FOR FAMILY ELEVATION

I release petty differences that block our family.

I release blocks and karma from our ancestors.

I release generational curses and cycles that block our family.

I honor my family and myself with my thoughts, words and actions.

I pray that our Ancestors are elevated and strong.

I pray that my Ancestors are pleased with us.

I pray that I become an honorable Ancestor and that I bring honor to my family.

I pray for our family to be elevated mentally, emotionally, physically, spiritually and financially.

I love my family as I love myself.

I want the best for my family and I want the best for myself.

Our family is strong, loving and healing.

So be it and so it is.

ANCESTRAL ELEVATION RITUAL

When a loved one makes their transition to the Ancestral Realm, it can be a difficult thing to process. We understand that our spirits live on beyond the physical realm as long as someone living speaks our name. We know that our ancestors can and do visit us and walk with us, even though we cannot see them. We also know that we should honor them and tell the stories to keep their energy alive within us and those who come after us.

If your loved one lived a good life and did not bring harm to themselves or others they can become elevated or honorable Ancestors. If not and they were harmful to themselves or others, mean spirited, evil, crazy or the like, they can not be helpful to the family and will not be elevated. When you call on your Ancestors you should only call the names of those who lived in a good and righteous way. In this world no one is perfect and everyone makes mistakes, however there is a difference between a good and not good person. For the ones who did not live righteously a candle can be lit and prayers made so they can find peace. This is also the case for those who die from suicide or accident, their names should not be called with those who are honorable.

There are some things that can be done to assist with the elevation of the righteous ancestors once they have crossed over. Here are a few spiritual things to be done when your loved one makes their transition to the Ancestral realm.

Directly after one makes their transition a prayer should be made and libation poured by those present to give honor and gratitude to the life of the new ancestor. This should be done next to the new ancestor.

PRAYER FOR ELEVATION OF THE ANCESTORS

We give thanks for the spirit and life of _____

Your work here has been good.

We are thankful and the ancestors are pleased.

We pray that your spirit will be at peace.

We pray that your spirit will be elevated and remembered

for years to come.

Go now and know that all is well.

May you be received well in the Ancestral Realm.

May you travel safely.

May your spirit be at peace.

We love you.

We thank you.

So be it and so it is!

This ritual can be done to assist your loved one with traveling to the ancestral realm. Wear white or light colors when you perform this ritual. It should be performed by the third day of ones transition.

This ritual can be done alone or in a group.

ITEMS NEEDED:

- White cloth for your altar
- Small table
- Crystals or a plant
- Picture of your loved one
- White seven day candle
- Any items from your loved one
- A glass or bowl of water
- Clear ammonia
- Lavender flowers or essential oil
- Florida water or rose water
- Frankincense & myrrh
- Charcoal and burning pot

THE RITUAL:

1. Make a mixture of spring water, Florida water (or rose water) ammonia and lavender. Use this mixture to spiritually cleanse the house. This will help to release any attachments that your loved one may have to the material world. Use a small cinnamon broom or sprinkle the water around the house with your hands. go into each room and sprinkle each corner of the rooms.

2. The house should be smudged with frankincense and myrrh going in a counter-clockwise direction to help release the energy of the person that has passed on. Every room, closet and corner of the house should be smudged. Use the Ancestral Elevation Prayer or say your own as you smudge the home.

3. You can create an altar for your loved one to help bring you peace. If you have an ancestor altar already you can add their picture of the to the one you already have. If you don't have an altar you can add one to your home to assist your ancestor in their elevation process and assist your family with healing and grieving.

4. Choose an area suitable for your ancestral altar, it should be in a more private area of your home so everyone who comes there would not see your altar.

5. Clean the area physically first, then add the table, cloth, bowl of water, plant picture and candle. Arrange the items in a way that feel good and balanced to you.

6. Light the candle and light your incense.

7. Say a prayer to your loved one and speak from your heart.

Send them love and peaceful energy. Cry, sing or meditate at your altar with your ancestors. Sit at the altar as long you need too.

8. Leave the altar up and take time to relax, process and rest.

CLOSING:

◊ Say a prayer of gratitude to your ancestors for the mediation and healing time.

◊ When the candle burns out completely, light another one or use a tea light candle. Keeping a candle lit for the first week is helpful. It is said that it will help your ancestor to go to the light. You can sit the burning candle in a bowl of water for safety if you feel you need too.

◊ You can add flowers, fruit, sweets or other items to this altar to feed the energy of your ancestor.

◊ Leave your altar up for a year or more.

◊ Change the water on the altar daily. Make sure to keep the altar clean and dust free.

◊ You can make prayers at your ancestral altar as often as you like. The more energy you give to your ancestors, the more energy they will give to you.

Prosperity Ritual

Prosperity and financial wealth are achieved through work, risk, dedication, sweat and being in the flow of abundance. Abundance moves in the energetic vibration of joy, harmony, peace and love. Without these things it can be difficult to achieve.

Using prosperity rituals, affirmations, reading books about financial wealth and changing your mindset are helpful in the process of acquiring financial wealth and healing your financial energy.

Prosperity Rituals can be done to increase wealth and finances. When done correctly they can bring a windfall of money or an increase in income immediately. Do as much work as you can to achieve wealth and prosperity. There is no magic wand to make you wealthy.

It is best to do prosperity rituals on Thursday or Friday and at new or full moon times. Choose affirmations to say during and after the ritual for best results.

Wear green or gold when your perform this ritual. It can be done alone or in a group.

Items Needed:
- Citrine, pyrite and/ or Malachite crystals
- Five green candles
- Three five dollar bills
- A handful of silver coins

- Jasmine, cinnamon or vanilla incense
- Green table cloth or material
- Gold dust, coins or chains
- Wine glass
- Fresh flowers (your choice)

THE RITUAL:

1. Create an altar on a small table with green material as a base. Decorate the table with the candles, the gold and the crystals.

2. Fill the wine glass with water and add a few drops of honey.

3. Light your incense and state your intentions.

4. Write a list of five things that you are grateful for and add it to the altar.

5. Write a list of the things or the amount of money that you desire. Write down the things you would do with the money you receive. Put your wishes on the altar.

6. Place the five dollar bills on top of the paper.

7. Place the candle on top of the bills and paper and light your green candle.

8. While you light the candle repeat the affirmations five times.

You can add your own affirmations and remember to use them again when you feel like you need to.

Prosperity Affirmations

I release anything that blocks me from being wealthy.

I am thankful for the increase in money, gold, silver, bitcoin and all that is coming to me.

Let financial wealth flow to me constantly and consistently from all directions.

I am financially healthy and wealthy.

9. . After saying the affirmations create a diamond shape crystal grid on the floor with the crystals and coins.

10. You can turn on binary tones or other meditative music.

12. Sit in the middle of the diamond crystal grid and prepare for your meditation.

Prosperity Meditation

Breathe deeply and relax.

Focus on your breath.

Breathe in through your nose and out through your mouth.

Allow your body to relax more and more with each breathe.

Visualize yourself outside in a magical forest.

There are trees and flowers everywhere.

You can smell the beautiful fragrance of the flowers as you breath in.

You can see birds and butterflies of all colors flying around you.

There is a waterfall ahead of you and you can feel the sprinkle of water hitting your skin.

It is a beautiful day full of life and abundance.

You feel a sense of gratitude and peace inside of you in this magical forest.

You begin to walk towards the waterfalls.

As you get closer you can see the water and the land around the water is golden.

It is a waterfall of gold coins, gems and jewels.

You can see wealth, prosperity and abundance all around you.

You go closer and begin to adorn yourself in the diamonds and gold.

You touch and feel the wealth of the universe all around you.

You become one with the energy of wealth and prosperity.

You feel the sun rays shining on you.

You feel a sense of joy and success overwhelming you.

You feel a sense of gratitude within you.

You know that you deserve to be wealthy.

You know that you can attract wealth, joy, beauty and love.

You fill you pockets and adorn your body with the jewels and wealth of the magical forest.

Give thanks and praises to the universe for sharing wealth and abundance with you.

Give thanks for the gifts and opportunities that are coming for you to get the wealth that you deserve.

Give thanks for the people that you will meet to assist you in your progress.

Take a deep breath and allow the feeling of peace, prosperity and joy fill your entire body.

Know that this is a part of you and you can be in this space at any time.

Take a deep breath and bring yourself back to your body.

Take another deep breath and return now to your sacred space.

Breathe deeply and when you are ready you can open your eyes.

Sit and relax as long as you need to .

13. Take your prosperity bath when you are ready.

Prosperity Bath

Items needed:

- Parsley
- Sage
- Bay leaves
- Rosemary
- Jasmine or honeysuckle oil
- One dollar cut into pieces.
- Rose water
- Yellow and red flowers
- Citrine or pyrite crystals

Add one tablespoon of each herb and other items to a metal, glass or wood bowl (don't use plastic).
As you add the items focus on the things that you want and need and speak your intentions into the bath.
Add the flower petals and some leaves do not add stems. Tear the petals into little pieces while you focus on joy, wealth and prosperity.
Add purified water to the bowl and say a prayer or say the affirmations as you mix everything together.
Use this to soak in or pour it over yourself after a shower.

This bath should be taken for five consecutive days after the ritual. You can repeat the bath as often as you like to encourage wealth and prosperity in your life.

Manifestation Ritual

We are all co-creators in our own life journey. Everything that was ever created begin with a thought. Then it is spoken out into the universe and then it becomes real in the physical realm. The process is still the same when it comes to manifestoing, things that we want in our life.

However we should understand that we must also match the vibrational frequency to receive what it is that we say we want. We are magnetic beings so we attract what we feel and think. If we are feeling at peace and living with love and joy we have a better chance of manifesting the good things that we want.

When we are living with fear, doubt, envy, anger or other negative emotion we will attract more of the same type of energy and experiences to create those same emotions. We have to learn to break the cycle of thinking and begin to realize and use our power. In doing so we will be able to truly live the life that we desire.

This ritual should be done on a special day numerically so a day like 3/3. 5/5. 6/6, 7/7 or 11/11 is known to be a power day. You can also choose to do the ritual on a full moon day. Time of day to start the ritual can be 5:00, 6:00, 7:00 or 9:00 am or pm.

This ritual can be done alone or in a group. Wear gold or magenta for best results.

ITEMS NEEDED:

- Magenta or gold tablecloth
- 2 Gold or purple candles
- Rose or frankincense incense
- Clear quartz, labradorite, citrine, topaz, pyrite, or malachite.
- Fresh flowers
- Binary tones of 432hz or higher

THE RITUAL:

1. Create an altar with the items listed and turn on your binary tones.
2. Arrange the items on the altar in a way that feels balanced and good to you.
3. Put a candle on each side of the table.
4. Add water to the glass and place on the altar.
5. Smudge space, the participants and yourself.
6. Libation
7. Write down ten things that you are thankful for.
8. Add this list to the Altar.
9. Say the Affirmation to Release Blocks and open the way for you to receive.

Affirmations for Manifestation

I release all blocks from by Ancestors

I release all blocks from past life times.

I release all blocks from my present time.

I release all karma from my Ancestors.

I release all negative karma from my past life times.

I release all negative karma from this life.

I release all oaths, bonds, ties and commitments from my Ancestors that do not serve me.

I release all oaths, bonds, ties and commitments from past lifetimes that do not serve me.

I release all oaths, ties, bonds, commitments from this life that no longer serve my highest good.

I attract the best that the Universe has for me.

I have everything that I want and need.

I am thankful for the rewards that are coming to me.

I deserve to receive the best of everything.

So be it and so it is!

10. Write down the things that you want and need. Be specific about everything that you write. Write in a petition style. (you can use the following example).

I_____(state your name)

Ask the Universe to bring me (write your list)

Thank you

So be it and so it is!

Make sure to sign your name at the bottom.

11. Read your list or speak what you want out to the Universe. Repeat it daily or as often as you like. When you are finished place your list on the altar.

12. Make a crystal grid on the floor with the crystals. Use a circle to represent the flow of life or choose a shape feels right to you.

13. When you are ready sit in a comfortable position and prepare for your meditation

MANIFESTING MEDITATION

Relax and breathe deeply.

Breath out through your mouth and in through your nose.

Take a few quick breaths in an out your nose (fire breaths).

Then return to deep breathing and allow yourself to settle down and relax even more.

Take a deep breath and visualize the color magenta.

A beautiful deep, bright pink ray of light swirling around you.

Breathe in the magenta light energy.

Feel it moving from up and down within your body.

Allow the magenta light energy to flow from your head to your toes.

The magenta light energy carries the vibration of manifestation.

As the energy flows through your body visualize the things that you want to manifest in front of you.

If it is a new house, see exactly the kind of house you want, see the neighborhood, size and color.

See yourself receiving the keys to your new house or car.

See yourself living there or driving the car wherever you want to go.

This is your dream and you can visualize it exactly the way you want it to be.

Allow your mind to see things s you desire them to be.

See yourself receiving all that you desire.

You are smiling, feeling happy and peaceful.

Know that you can have everything that you want.

Know that you deserve to have all that you desire.

Breathe deeply and continue to dream as long as you need to.

Remember the feeling and the visualizations that you had.

Give thanks to the Ancestors and Universe for making your dreams come true.

Take a deep breath.

When you are ready you can open your eyes.

Sit and relax as long as you need to.

CLOSING:

- After the meditation, say a prayer of gratitude to the Guides and to the Universe for assistance.

- Allow the candles to burn until they burn out completely.

- Leave the altar up for five, seven, nine or eleven days.

- Take a bath or shower and relax or write in your journal after the ritual. The prosperity bath is good to use to assist with your manifestations.

Hex/Spell Breaker Ritual

A spell, hex or curse is a negative energy that is sent from one to another. It can be as simple as jealousy, envy or the evil eye. It can also be the consistent negative thoughts from one to another. Finally they can be sent by someone who knows root work, hoodoo, voodoo, magic or witchcraft. The latter case is the most difficult to break, but not impossible.

If you are a person with a strong aura and strong spiritual connection you will not be affected by most spells and curses that ones may try to send to you.

If you are a person with a weak aura and not living with integrity or full of fear and doubt, you can be affected by the words and negative energy of others.

If you are feeling like you have a streak of bad luck or things are not going your way all of a sudden it could be due to a curse, hex or other witchcraft from an outside source or being.

There are many books to give instructions for many spells, however the law of reciprocity states that everything you do will come back to you and that includes black magic and casting spells against others.

In fact any manipulation of another person's will or the wishing of harm to others can and will attract malevolent and mischievous forces that will want payment for such services.

If you feel like you may have been cursed you can do this ritual to help clear the karma and break the spell. It is best to do this on a Friday or Saturday during a full moon or waning moon.

Wear white and do this ritual alone.

ITEMS NEEDED:
* 3 black candles
* Dragons blood incense
* Plain paper
* Red pen or marker
* Black tourmaline or other black stones
* Charcoal and container to burn it in safely (metal container)

THE RITUAL:
1. Create a small altar with a white table cloth.

2. Draw a circle with a cross in the middle of the paper with the red pen.

3. Put the paper in the middle of the alter.

4. Place the black stones on the outside of the page with one in each of the four directions.

5. Place a black candle in the middle of the circle. Make sure to wash the candle and remove any stickers.

6. Light the dragon's blood incense and then light the candle.

7. Say these words or something similar seven times.

> *I release all curses, spells and negative energy that others have put out against me and I return it back to its sender.*

8. Let the candle burn until it burns out completely then light the next one and repeat the process until you have burned all three candles. You should feel lighter when this is done.

9. While the candles are burning you can make a spiritual bath for yourself and your home with the listed ingredients.

10. Mix all ingredients together in a small bowl with bottle water. Take a portion of the mixture and set aside for your personal spiritual bath.

11. Take part of the mixture around the inside of your home and sprinkle the bath on the floors, walls, and corners of each room. Move in a counter-clockwise direction to take the energy away.

12. Command that all negative energy leave your home. Release

any spells, curses or other negative forces that may be active in your home.

13. Once you feel complete plan to take your spiritual bath. It is best for you to soak in the tub for this bath.

Hex Breaker Spiritual Bath

Items Needed:

* Bay leaves
* Clear ammonia
* Rosemary leaves
* Florida water
* Hibiscus flowers
* Red flowers
* Cinnamon
* Rose oil
* Dragons blood incense

Run the water until the bath is half full, the water should be lukewarm not hot. Add the spiritual bath mixture and soak in the tub for 20—30 minutes.

Speak out and release all that does not serve you into the tub. Visualize a red and golden light surrounding you and protecting you.

Relax and meditate as long as you need to. When you are ready get off and dress in white clothes.

14. Your next step is to create a seal of protection around your home. If you live in an apartment you can go around the building or just walk around your apartment. You will take the remaining part of the bath in a clockwise direction around the outside of your home and create a force field or a shield of protection that surrounds your home that nothing or no one can penetrate. Pray that no hurt or harm can come to your door. This will create a grid of protection around your house that will protect the house and everyone in it.

CLOSING:

- Once this is done and all candles have burned out relax and know that it is done.
- There will be subtle and sometimes drastic shifts in your life. Just go with the flow and know that all is well and moving in divine order.

Any doubts or fears that you have will work against you so feel confident in the ritual and your power.

- Give thanks to the Warriors for assisting you with the process.
- Keep the altar up for three weeks at least.
- You can always get more candles and repeat the process again if you feel that it is necessary.

Freedom Ritual

The prison system is one of the most wicked and corrupt systems in this country. When one is locked in a cage for years it will condition and change the energy, mind, body and spirit of the person. They are not the same person whether they committed the crime they are accused of or not. Time spent under those conditions can be traumatizing to say the least. Family support, counseling, spiritual work and rituals can be helpful to bring healing and balance to those who have been traumatized by those circumstances.

Oftentimes when a person is released from prison they commit another crime and return to prison within months of them getting released. They are unable to re-enter the community in a way that will support their growth and development. It can take years for someone to readjust to society after being imprisoned for a long period of time.

Having some spiritual assistance to clear the negative energy from their auric field and give them a true feeling of being refreshed and renewed. Spiritual connection can be helpful for their journey of adjustment back into society with more balance and harmony.

This ritual is for those have been released from prison or jail. It is meant to assist one with being in gratitude for liberation from the penal system, to help clear away negative energy that may be with them and to help with readjusting to life in a spiritual way.

THE RITUAL:

1. When one is released from jail or prison the first thing they should do is turn around 7 times counter-clockwise to break the ties and connection to the prison system.

2. These affirmations can also be said upon release.

AFFIRMATIONS FOR FREEDOM

I give thanks and praises to the Most High for my freedom.
I give thanks and praises to my Ancestors for my freedom.
I ask for forgiveness for all that I have done.
I forgive myself and others who have hurt me.
I pray that my heart and mind can find peace.
I am free of the bonds and ties of the system.
I am free from the past.
I give thanks for my life and for all things great and small.
Amen (Ase)

3. Next the aura should be cleared using three eggs. Start at the head and roll the eggs, one at a time over your entire body

4. Throw the eggs away from the house to break them when finished. If possible do this at a park or the woods.

5. Smudging should be done with frankincense, myrrh, benzoin, and dragon's blood. Smudging can be done everyday for two to four weeks.

6. A series of spiritual baths should be taken everyday if possible for thirty days or more. (about thirty to fifty spiritual baths) This will help to shift the energy from bondage to freedom.

SPIRITUAL BATH FOR FREEDOM

ITEMS NEEDED:
- ◊ Peroxide
- ◊ Baking soda
- ◊ Florida water
- ◊ Frankincense oil
- ◊ 3 lemons
- ◊ Lemon balm or lemongrass oil
- ◊ Coconut milk or nut milk

Add the items to a metal, glass or wood bowl (don't use plastic).
As you add the items think love and forgiveness and put your intentions into the bath.
Focus on releasing negativity and adding your intentions for your future to your bath.
Add purified water to the bowl and say a prayer or say the Freedom affirmations as you mix everything together.
Use this to soak in or pour it over yourself after a shower.
Say the affirmations or your own prayer as you take the bath.

Spiritual baths should be done on Monday, Friday or Sunday, or everyday if possible. Soaking in the tub is very helpful but the shower method will work.

While taking the bath meditate on releasing the negative energy from the past and clearing the way for your future.

Speak out everything that you want to let go of and visualize that energy going down the drain with the water.

Ask for forgiveness for your mistakes and shortcomings and forgive yourself. Speak from your heart and allow your heart to heal and change.

7. After your bath wear white or light colors and just relax, no TV or outside influences if possible. Just connect with your true self.

PART TWO - MAKE OFFERINGS

Making offerings is a way of giving back to the Ancestral and Spiritual forces that have given to you. As you give you also receive. Making offerings can also help to balance your karma.

When you can, make offerings to your ancestors. If you have done something to offend your ancestors it is in your best interest to make amends to them. Offer sweet things like honey, perfume, flowers, candy, cake, fruit, etc.... you can take the offerings for them to a graveyard, just give it to a tree if your ancestors are not buried there .

- Give offerings at the ocean where some of our ancestors perished during the middle passage.

- Give offering to ancestors out in an open field. Pour libation, call their names and leave the food on a white paper plate or directly on the ground.

- When you give to your ancestors be sure to ask them to forgive you, apologize for your behavior and thank them for being with your and allowing you to make it home alive. Speak from your heart and talk to your great grandparents about your feelings and concerns. Know that they are with you and they can hear you.

- Make offerings to them daily or at least once a week to strengthen your relationship and make amends with them.

PART THREE CREATE A GRATITUDE JOURNAL

- Buy a notebook to write your gratitude list.

- Write ten things you are thankful for everyday. If you forget a day just pickup the next day and keep going. Having an attitude of gratitude is very healing to the heart and spirit.

There is always something to be thankful for.

PART FOUR—PRAYER AND MEDITATION

Prayer and meditation help to raise your vibration from the lower self to the higher self. Having a daily prayer or chanting schedule will help to put your thoughts in a higher consciousness.

Read positive books and pray at least three time each day to help you shift your energy in a positive direction. Praying often will help you reconnect with the Most High and your Spirit Guides so you can live a better life, make better choices and live a more positive life.

◊ Light a white tea light candle each morning when you do your prayers. The energy of fire is transforming and can help in your transformation and healing process.

◊ When you light the candle say a positive affirmation to assist in reprograming your mind.

◊ Say the 42 Laws of Maat, the Ten Commandments or a prayer to help you reprogram your thoughts and ways of living. This will help you to shift your mind to a higher state of consciousness. It will also teach you to hold yourself accountable for your actions. When you fall short of the laws you can always make amends to atone and balance out your karma in some way.

Taking these steps will create more peace and balance in your life so you can have a fresh start mentally, emotionally and spiritually. It is meant to help your enjoy the benefits of true freedom.

Final Thoughts

These rituals are meant to assist you on your healing journey. There is no magic wand for healing. It takes work, dedication, energy, time, self-realization, self-reflection, releasing emotions, and discipline to heal. Everyone does it in their own time and everything does not always work for everyone.

Healing is a lifetime, daily process. The more energy you put towards your healing, the better and more balanced you will feel. When you can speak about something without crying or getting emotional about it, you know that healing has started.

Everyone's journey is different and most importantly, it is about respecting and honoring the process. Honor your own healing process and journey. Do what you feel is best for you, as there is no one who can tell you what is best for you better than yourself.

We create with our thoughts and our words so we can use that power to help us heal.

We pray this information will be helpful to you and that you will experience true and complete healing of your mind, your body and your spirit If you need assistance, you can reach out to us at rasekhitemple@gmail.com or visit us online for information about our healing classes and products.

This publication was designed to provide helpful information in regard to the subject matters covered. It is sold with the intention to educate, inform and empower readers to make their own decisions on health and well being. If you have concerns about your physical, mental or emotional condition consult the appropriate professional.

Also by Ra Sekhi Arts Temple

Ra Sekhi Kemetic Reiki Level 1

Kemetic Reiki Level 2

Recipes for Elevation

Speaking with Spirit

Sekhmet Rising

A Nation Rising

I Get Energy From the Sun

Light as a Feather

I am Mind, Body & Spirit

Books are available at www.rasekhistore.com

And Amazon

Also visit us at

Www.rasekhihealing.com

Www.rasekhi.bandcamp.com

Www.payhip.com/rasekhitemple

Www.youtube.com/rasekhitemple

www.ingramcontent.com/pod-product-compliance
Lightning Source LLC
Chambersburg PA
CBHW010449010526
44118CB00019B/2518